A Visit to
Oaklenbrooke Farm

Aleigha C. Israel

illustrated by Mariposa Aristeo

This adventure is presented to

_____

by _____

on _____

"Sister and I are going to Oaklenbrooke Farm,
I can hardly stand the wait. Let's hurry and
get ready, it wouldn't do to be late."

"So, grab your lunch, your hat, and a coat.
We'll go visit the pigs, cows, sheep and a goat."

"For you see all these animals were made with such care.
Are you ready? Set, go! I'll beat you there!"

"Do you see that silly donkey with his funny sounding bray? That goat looks so smart, if he could talk what would he say?"

"Look at that dirty pig. What a mess.
Oh no. Watch out. He slung some on your dress!"

"Let's head on over to the giant red barn.
Away from mud-slinging pigs—though I doubt he meant harm!"

"Do you smell that hay? It's so fresh and sweet. Let's stop for a break. Are you ready to eat?"

"Did you know that pigs have 44 teeth? Or that cows have 4 stomachs, now isn't that neat?"

"I'm done with my lunch, are you finished with yours?
Let's see if the farmer will let us help with the chores."

"After placing fresh hay in the hen's nesting box,
let's head on over to the pond, by the old boat dock."

"Do you see that mother duck with her ducklings in a row?
That pony is headed straight for us! Whoa, pony whoa!"

"Phew, we're ok, but oh, that was close! If we hadn't moved fast he would have stepped on our toes!"

"Oh, look at the sun, it's time to start back. If we head on home now, we can walk the old train track."

"Now wasn't today fun?
What was your favorite part?
I still think that goat looked so very smart."

"I'm glad you came along, it wouldn't have been half so much fun alone.
But we know one thing for sure, it's that there's no place like home."

The End

FUN FARM FACTS

Fun Cow Facts

1. Cows can see almost **360** degrees. This near-panoramic view lets them watch for predators from all angles. However, they don't see well straight in front of them so they will typically turn their head to look at you.
2. Cows have **4** stomaches.

Fun Pig Facts

1. Did you know that, contrary to what most people think, pigs are actually quite clean? This misconception comes from the fact that pigs that live in hot climates roll around in mud to cool off.
2. Pigs are one of the smartest domesticated animals – and are actually smarter than dogs!

Fun Horse Facts

1. Horses have around **205** bones in their skeleton.
2. Horses have bigger eyes than any other mammal that lives on land.

Fun Sheep Facts

1. A sheep's fur is called "wool" and people use it to make clothes! **1** pound of wool can make up to **10** miles of yarn.
2. George Washington, Thomas Jefferson and James Madison all raised sheep. In fact, Madison was sworn in wearing a coat spun from his sheep's wool.

Funny Farm Jokes

Q: What do ducks put in their soup?
A: Quackers.

Q: What dog loves to take bubble baths?
A: A shampoodle!

Q: What's louder than a dog barking outside your window?
A: Two dogs barking outside your window.

Q: What do you call a sheep with no legs.
A: A cloud.

Q: What did the horse say when it fell?
A: I've fallen and I can't giddyup!

Q: What time is it when a cow sits on your hat?
A: Time to get a new hat!

Q: What do you call a sleeping cow?
A: A bull dozer.

Q: What do you call a dancing sheep?
A: A baa-lerina!

Q: What do cows do in their spare time?
A: Listen to moooosic.

Q: What do you call a sheep covered in chocolate?
A: A Candy Baa.

Q: What do you call a pig with no legs?
A: A groundhog.

Q: What did the duck say to the waiter when the check came?
A: Put it on my bill please.

Q: What did the pig say when he got hurt?
A: Call the hambulance!

About the Author

Hi!

My name is ALEIGHA C. ISRAEL and I write inspirational fiction and poetry.
I'm an author of multiple books and enjoy sharing God's love through the powerful art of storytelling.

I love being a Community Assistant at the Young Writers Workshop and
teaching writing classes to my talented students!

When I'm not daydreaming about a new story idea or playing with my sidekick "Marley" (a Pomeranian mix)
I can usually be seen traveling with my family's gospel bluegrass band, "Fret Not" or making
personalized author swag for my business *Literary Treasures*.

I don't have to search very hard for inspiration.

Living in the Israel household, it's guaranteed there's an adventure waiting around every corner!

For more information about me and my books, you can visit my website ALEIGHACISRAEL.COM

About the Illustrator

Mariposa Aristeo is a self-taught artist and writer who captures the glories of God's creation on paper.

She is the Graphic, Instagram, and Email Manager at Story Embers, where she encourages storytellers in crafting novels that ignite the imagination and warm the heart.

As a reclusive INFJ, she enjoys quiet activities such as hiding Easter eggs in her art, perusing Charles Spurgeon books, and burning spiders at the stake.

She hopes to someday publish her own children's book, a kooky tale that combines humor, heart, and her longtime love of dinosaurs. Her fictional assistant, Aberdeen the Authorosaurus (an ink-drinking, book-eating dinosaur), supplies her with most of her story ideas and forces her to write by threatening to sit on her.

If you want to read about his exploits in her office, writerly dinosaurian advice, or nonsensical sense, please visit: www.dinosdigest.com or his Instagram page, @aberdeentheauthorosaurus.

www.ingramcontent.com/pod-product-compliance
Lightning Source LLC
Chambersburg PA
CBHW040405100426

42811CB00017B/1844